Great Thoughts

From a

Little Dog

MARGARET PEAT

Acknowledgements

Thank you to Kevin, my partner in dog walking and also in life. My greatest gift ever!

Special thanks to David and Jan Holdaway for your expertise, excellence and never ending patience in helping me bring this book to fruition.

Copyright © 2012 Margaret Peat

Scripture taken from the *New King James Version.*

Definitions taken from *The New Oxford School Dictionary.* OUP. Joyce M Hawkins.

Cover design by Graham Alder

Contact: email: KMPeat@aol.com

Life Publications

Commendations

Having had cats and dogs all my life, I know there's a world of difference between these two household pets. It has rightly been said that dogs have masters and cats have staff. Dogs are eager to please and obey; cats are aloof and independent. In this respect, dogs have so much to teach us about how we relate to God and how God, our Heavenly Dad, relates to us. So sit up straight, prick up your ears, wag your tail, stick out your tongue – you are about to get seriously well fed!

Dr Mark Stibbe, Founder of *Father's House Trust.* Mark ministered as Senior Minister of St Andrew's Chorley Wood for many years and is currently Founder and Director of Fathers House Trust. He is also proud owner of 'Molly.'

Margaret Peat has written an entertaining and inspiring devotional. Whether you are a tenacious bull dog or pampered pouch, it offers healing to the heart that is open.

Amanda Dye, married to Colin Dye, senior leader of Kensington Temple, London, and is the proud owner of 'Branquela' and 'Simba.'

As a veterinary surgeon for fourteen years I have seen how the love of pet owners goes beyond ownership and delves further into the soul of people to create a totally so-called irrational state of love, service, adoration and a willingness to break all normal boundaries for the sake of the new member of the family. Whether it's a doey-eyed Labrador, a bouncy Spaniel or the motionally challenged Retriever, dogs cause things to happen in humans that are deep.

Margaret has linked the fun and devoted side of knowing 'man's best friend' to the, at times, completely irrational way God sees and loves us. This book will bring a smile to your face and a longing in your heart for more of Him. God will meet you through this book.

Stuart Glassborow, B.Vet.Med. M.R.C.V.S Stuart has practised as a Veterinarian Surgeon for many years and is also Senior Pastor of Catch the Fire, Wembley. He is the proud owner of 'Baloo.'

What a delightful little devotional. With being a dog lover and owner of many different breeds of dog over 45 years, I could identify with so much of each daily reading. It never ceases to amaze me of how faithful a dog is to his master the same way God our Master is always so faithful to us. Margaret's creative writing style captivates your mind bringing memories of past canines that had become members of our family, and Chester our current member.

She is an inspirational author and I always enjoy reading her books and also catching up with her on visits to New Zealand.

Marilyn Brough, married to Luke Brough, Senior Pastor of Elim Christian Centre Howick, Auckland, New Zealand. (Previous General Superintendent of Elim New Zealand). She is also proud owner of 'Chester.'

Dedication

This book is dedicated to our Heavenly Father who in his amazing kindness created 'the dog' for us to enjoy.

Then God said, Let the earth bring forth the living creature according to its kind: cattle and creeping thing and beast of the earth, each according to its kind; and it was so. And God made the beast of the earth according to its kind, cattle according to its kind, and everything that creeps on the earth according to its kind.

And God saw that it was good.

Genesis 1:24,25

Contents

Introduction

We have always owned a dog. As a child, my husband Kevin, shared a house with Susie and Rex, black and golden labradors respectively and I grew up beside Jock, a rumbustious mongrel full of life and vigour.

When we got married, within days we knew our home would not be complete without a dog lying in front of the fire and so our adventure began.

For ten years we were graced by the presence of Michael, our first dog and a truly awesome little fellow who watched us hear the call of God and move from our home town to Glasgow, Scotland. For a wonderful seventeen years, we were then accompanied by Mary who was totally mad and manic until she was seven years old, but who grew into a loving, faithful and wonderful friend. She was with us as we built our first church and through all that life in the ministry entailed in those days.

And then Jak Mac Peat came into our lives.

If you love dogs, then I hope you will like this book and through the anecdotes about our current dog Jak, that something in it will draw you nearer to God. I write unashamedly for dog lovers and for God lovers.

This book is about your inward journey. It is devotional in character and, based on the book of Psalms, it explores the blessings of knowing the Father for yourself and all that He can pour into your life. There are questions to contemplate, prayers to pray, Psalms to meditate on and where the Psalms develop that theme, further study to do if you have time. Through it, I hope you will experience more of God's provision to you personally, in order that you can put it to work in the world to which He has called you.

I hope too that you, as a God lover or as a dog lover, will somehow find your way deeper into the Father's love. It will not only improve your life, it will change it forever.

1

You Are *Provided For*

(Provide = make something available; supply)

I remember the day that Jak Mac Peat came into our lives. Mary, who was our much beloved previous dog, had been put to sleep some six months before and I was praying hard for another dog. But the routine at our current stage of life meant that we were away from home a lot, so another dog (according to Kevin) was out of the question.

That was until that magical, wonderful day, when an old friend rang me. She had acquired a puppy a couple of weeks before and after two weeks of sleepless nights, rain sodden walks and much puddle cleaning of the floor, she felt that a puppy and her hectic lifestyle just didn't go together.

"It's worse than a baby," she said and her next statement delighted me intensely for suddenly, I could see God making a way where there was no way!

"You have my puppy and I'll be available to look after it whenever and however long you need me. I'll see wee Mac..." (his name was

Mac then), "...but without providing long term care, training, food, walks, accommodation and vets visits!" (And of course she forgot to mention the sleepless nights, rain sodden walks and floor cleaning too!) It worked for us both! How great is our God.

Later that night, I sat and imagined him, in typical puppy fashion, racing round our home and garden, running, jumping up, chewing and growling and then suddenly dropping to the floor. His eyes would be closing, fighting to stay awake and continue the game but eventually he would give in and end in a heap, fast asleep in the most unusual places. The corner of the bathroom, a shoebox, the fireplace or the compost heap would become a very comfortable sleeping place for an hour or so until the adventure began all over again. "God is so good," I thought as I dropped off to sleep that night. Yes, God is so good.

****

Yes, how great is our God. Whatever you are facing, He can and He will make a way where there is no way. It may not be the way you would have chosen, or planned or expected. Then again, it may be exactly what you have dreamed. But He will make a way for you through any and every situation in which you find yourself. Sometimes, He calls you to look at that 'obstacle' and with the hammer and chisel of your own will, turn it into an 'altar'. Then that very thing which stood in your way, becomes the very place which brings you closer to God. Remember, He will make a way for you where there is no way.

Question:

What situation in your life do you need God to make a way through today? Are you prepared for it to be His way?

Prayer:

Take time to thank Him now, that however He works things, He will make a way where there is no way.

Meditation:

Psalm 37:23-25 *The steps of a good man are ordered by the Lord, and He delights in his way. Though he fall, he shall not be utterly cast down; for the Lord upholds him with His hand. I have been young, and now am old; Yet I have not seen the righteous forsaken, nor his descendants begging for bread.*

Other:

Psalm 23:1, 23:5, 34:10, 37:5, 104:14-15, 104:28, 127:2, 147:14

Further study:

You are *Granted:* Psalm 20:4-5

Notes:

2

You Are *Delighted In*

(Delight = please someone greatly, feel great pleasure)

The day had finally arrived!

On the Friday morning I woke like a child at Christmas and counted the hours through the day. By 6.30pm, I had rung at least five people to let them know of the impending arrival of my new little animal! Eventually, at 7.30pm little Mac arrived, a bundle of fur on legs!

After being introduced to his new bed, a whole host of toys, a new ball, one short and one extending lead, a treat ball, a puppy cage, a packet of chew sticks, a wee mat and a set of poo bags, so began the rest of his life as Peat!

What would I call him? 'Jak Mac Peat' would be perfect! A perfect name for a perfect little dog. I looked at him across the room as he had recently collapsed in an exhausted heap after his twenty minute trip from Glasgow. I thought of the coming years of this poo-eating, tail-chasing, bottom-sniffing little dog.

A small and helpless creature with big irresistible eyes, be it human or animal, creates an irrational attraction which I knew this creature would take advantage of big time. I also knew that he would exploit my compulsive 'anthropomorphizing' to the maximum extent.

Jak was a Borkie, half Bishon, half Yorkie but out of four hundred breeds of dogs, he couldn't be more perfect.

****

You know, the excitement I felt over my puppy, is absolutely, totally and unequivocally *nothing,* compared to the excitement your Father in Heaven feels every time you come to Him. He *loves* to spend time with you. You may or may not have known or experienced a human father's love but if you belong to Him, you have someone who passionately loves you. Not because of what you've done or not done for Him, but because you are His boy or His girl, and that's all that matters. I had no history with Jak Mac Peat. But Friday 7.30pm, I loved him because he was mine. When you join God's family, you become His child and He is crazy over you. Not your brother, spouse, parent, friend or child, but over you!

How special, to have a father like that?

Question:

Are you fully aware of God's feelings towards you? Do you need to explore this more?

Prayer:

Ask Him to take His Father's love deeper into your heart and understanding today, then take time to let Him do it.

Meditation:

Psalm 149:4 *For the Lord takes pleasure in his people. He will beautify the humble with salvation.*

Other:

Psalm 147:11

Further study:

You are *Cared For:* Psalm 26:3, 27:10, 103:8, 117:2, 145:8-9

You are *Loved:* Psalm 92:2, 103:4, 107:31, 107:43, 144:2, 146:8

Notes:

3

You are *Safe*

(Safe = free from risk or danger)

When we had Michael, our first dog, we lasted two nights before he joined us in the bedroom through the night. With our second dog, Mary, we lasted two hours and with wee Jak Mac Peat, it was all of two minutes. Jak slept at the side of the bed in a homemade dog-run between the bed and the wall, with a temporary cat carrier at the end to stop an early hours escape.

At half past six in the morning, I stirred and just couldn't resist a peep at our new little animal. I leaned over the side of the bed and looked into the cat box. No Jak! I looked along the rest of the space between wall and bed. No Jak!

Where was the dog? Somehow, in some way, although we both deny knowledge of it, he had managed to end up on the end of the bed and was beautifully arranged between a stuffed lion and a teddy bear. Our tiny black and white puppy looked up with those vulnerable and sleepy eyes and at that moment, he knew and I knew that there was no way he was going back on the floor.

Half an hour later, I carried him down the stairs in a 'leak-avoiding' manner! The weather in Scotland can be cruel and that morning, I stood in the doorway watching the wind blow and the rain fall while he took his early morning duty. I wanted to scoop him up and bring him back inside but I knew he needed to stay there and do what needed to be done!

****

How many times have you felt that God has picked you up and dumped you outside in the rain and wind? How many times have you been snug and warm in everyday life and felt you've been rudely awoken and left in gale force winds? You may even be there right now?

Whenever it may have been or may be, you need to know that your God stands at that patio door and He watches over you. Sometimes, big black rooks used to land on the fence and surround my dog. But Jak Mac Peat was safe because I was watching.

And whatever you face whenever it may be, your God is there for you. Of course He wants to scoop you up and bring you inside but He knows you need to remain and learn. But rest assured, in His perfect time and way, He will do just that. He will bring you through. And until then, you are safe, for He watches over you.

Question:

Think back over your life thus far. Name some specific times when you have been in that place of wind and rain, longing for God to remove you from the situation?

Prayer:

Take time to talk to Him about those times when you have been out in the storm. Acknowledge His presence in your life just now. Walk by faith not feeling and thank Him that He is by your side and you are safe in that fact.

Meditation:

Psalm 4:8 *I will lie down and sleep peacefully, for you, Lord, make me safe and secure.*

Other:

Psalm 9:9, 14:6, 91:2, 91:4-6,

Further study:

You are *Defended:* Psalm 5:11, 18:47, 20:1, 59:9, 62:2, 62:6, 94:22, 140:12

You are *Hidden:* Psalm 32:7, 27:5, 31:20, 57:1, 59:16

You are *Protected:* Psalm 3:3, 18:30, 28:7-8, 33:20, 34:20, 36:7, 61:3-4, 91:4, 91:11-12, 91:14, 94:22, 107:41, 115:9, 121:3-8, 144:1-2, 145:20, 146:9

You are *Preserved:* Psalm 31:23, 32:7, 40:11

You are *Sheltered:* Psalm 91.1, 91.4, 144.2

You are *Surrounded:* Psalm 32.7, 32.10, 34.7

Notes:

4

You are *Forgiven*

(Forgive = To stop feeling angry with someone about something)

We all make mistakes. And Jak Mac Peat made plenty! Have you every tried to house train a puppy? Stuffed toys are so much easier to train! 'Wee after sleep, play and food' they say. Puppies are like a leaky stuffed toy, anywhere and everywhere!

We worked hard using the puppy mats and I thought we were having great success until one day, I'd spent twenty minutes standing with the dog in the wind and rain, waiting for even some sign of hope. Eventually, after no result I took him home where he immediately went and relieved himself grandly on the puppy mat I'd taught him to wee on!

"Don't reprimand unless caught in the act," the books say. And yet, ages later, whenever I found a little pool or a little pile, I'd pick him up and take him over, say nothing at all but nevertheless feel him stiffen and his little paws cling onto my arm in case I brought him nearer to his 'sin'

For a tiny dog, I seemed to do an incredibly high percentage of 'poop scooping' and there were definitely times that we felt we needed to invest in a gas mask! Training in these matters must be quite confusing to a dog when you consider it: When outside, owners wait excitedly for 'the event' to take place. They then warmly congratulate the dog on their achievement, appear to study the dog's deposit in detail then carefully collect the specimen in a sealed bag ready for who knows what? As that event was so successful, the little fellow then spends the rest of the evening straining again to please his owners, only to receive a completely opposite reaction when he succeeds on the new carpet!

'How to play' must be confusing too! It seems that chasing balls around the carpet is on whilst chasing fruit around the kitchen worktop is off. Chasing a stuffed cat around the house is on but chasing a cat that actually miaows is definitely off!

Eating must also be interesting. It's amazing how nice everything seems to taste to a puppy, and if the owner happens to have written on it or if it can be spent at the local store, this seemed to give it an added flavour somehow!

There were many things for Jak Mac Peat to get wrong, yet the funny thing was, whether he was right or wrong, I loved him none the less, because I knew he was learning and growing and changing. In fact, thinking about it, in his mistakes I loved him all the more!

****

We all make mistakes and you have a God whose love is unconditional. Today, be assured that whatever you do, wherever you go, He is there to guide you back onto the right path. Whenever you fail, whether in thought, word, deed or attitude, He loves you none the less. You are His child and you are on a journey. Yes, it is His desire that we aim for His highest and we do that because we love Him. He wants you to succeed and when you come to Him in repentance, He is ever present with His forgiving grace to pick you up and lead you further and higher for His glory.

Question:

What pools or piles have you made recently in thought, word, deed or attitude?

Prayer:

Bring these things before God and tell Him you are sorry. Truly ask Him to forgive you and to cleanse you afresh.

Meditation:

Psalm 86:5 *For you, Lord, are good, and ready to forgive, and abundant in mercy to all those who call upon you.*

Other:

Psalm 32:1, 32:5, 103:3, 103:12

Further study:

You are *Shown Mercy:* Psalm 111.4, 116.5

23

Notes:

5

You are *Helped*

(Help = to do part of another person's work for him or her benefit; make something better or easier)

And so began the life of Jak as a Peat.

"Brush fur weekly if short. Brush fur daily if long," say the books. Jak's fur wasn't quite that of the longest Yorkie in history which was two feet long, but certainly it also didn't qualify as short. Being a cross between a 'Bishon' with its curls and a 'Yorkie' with its length of hair, the fur definitely needed attention.

And as if to enhance the experience, from time to time he would not come home alone but would arrive with a few squatters too! We would work hard to evict them, but sooner or later, the incessant scratching both day and night, would signal the need for a doggie bubble bath-time. Our previous dog, Mary, loved the water, and would find her way into any and every puddle we found on a walk but it seemed that Jak had no more love for water than most cats do.

But bath time had to come sooner or later and when it did, it never failed to amaze us, how it took both of us, suitably clad in old tee shirts and shorts, sporting a total weight of anywhere over 25 stones, to submerge a mere 5lb of dog into a bath of water!

Once the bathroom door was shut, the deed was eventually done and sooner or later, the three of us emerged from the room bedraggled and exhausted, but triumphant, and most important of all, flee-less! Not even one lone squatter remaining!

It was amazing though, that no matter how well we towelled him dry, one little dog, on his first shake seemed to manufacture enough water to fill the River Clyde!

****

Your God is ever present to help you. Whatever your situation, be it peaceful or stressful, He wants to be involved in every part of your life to enable to you to run further, fly higher and swim deeper. He wants to be your helper and as you serve Him, He is close beside you through any and every circumstance to help.

Question:

What does your day entail? Will you let Him help you in that?

Prayer:

Bring those things before Him and thank Him that whenever you call Him, He will always be there for you.

Meditation:

Psalm 46:1 *God is our refuge and strength, a very present help in trouble.*

Other:

Psalm 20:2, 28:7-8, 33:20, 37:40, 40:17, 54:4, 63:7, 70:5, 94:17, 115:9, 118:7, 118:13, 121:2

Further study:

Now select more Bible verses which promise help from above, in some way to you.

Notes:

6

You Are *Comforted*

(Comfort = to make a person less unhappy; soothe)

Every dog has its sob story...getting left outside in a thunder storm, a disagreement with next door's cat or a long lost favourite toy.

The experts say that 'fear imprinting' occurs most often between five and ten weeks old and I knew that Jak was well past that age but even so, I was careful in those first few months to make sure that most of his experiences were positive ones. He was growing into a confident little dog, 'a big personality in a little package' as they say about the 'Yorkie' half of him, but if he ever sensed something was not right or strange, then he'd come and hang around me, not wanting me to know he was concerned but there all the less. On those occasions, I tried not to comfort him as I knew that sympathy would only reinforce the fear so I acted nonchalant and light hearted so he could see there was nothing to be anxious about. That was until that fateful morning when the big red monster appeared.

It was a cold morning, more so than usual and I'd left the heating off the night before. Jak was just finishing the third chase of his tail which he'd recently discovered to be constantly following him around, always ready for a good time. Completing that activity, he was now on the prowl for some new adventure. Should he dig up the blue plastic bone he'd buried in the settee yesterday or should he have a sleep even though he'd been awake only twenty five minutes? He appeared to decide on the latter and pattered into the lounge to choose a nice comfy cushion on which to settle.

And then, he saw it! A huge, red, glowing dragon was standing between the wall and the chair, watching *him!* In an instant, he was no longer Jak Mac Peat of East Kilbride, but Sir Galahad the Glorious saving the household from certain death and destruction.
That was until the monster bit him hard on the nose! I heard the yelp and rushed from my bowl of cornflakes in the kitchen to the halogen heater in the lounge and a small defenceless, very deflated little Sir Galahad trembling behind the sofa. In an instant, I bent and scooped the trembling bundle up into the air, high above what seemed like powers and principalities below.

It was a painful one, but a lesson well learned, as he never went near the monster again!

****

Some things in life really hurt. Not the frequent small happenings, but from time to time we all get hit with something big: a bereavement, a redundancy, a health situation or whatever. And when we do, it's difficult to see beyond that issue. It's hard to feel anything but the pain. But at those times, it's good to be reminded that He is ever ready to visit us with His comforting arms, to soothe and to restore. That is His promise to you.

Question:

Which would be the very first 'halogen heater' to bite you on the nose? Have you allowed God to lift you above that and deal with the effects in your life?

Prayer:

Bring these things before God and ask Him to pour His healing ointment onto those painful areas.

Meditation:

Psalm 94:19 *In the multitude of my anxieties within me, your comforts delight my soul.*

Other:

Psalm 23:4, 34:4, 86:17

Further study:

Now select more Bible verses which speak about God's comfort to every child of His.

Notes:

7

You are *Energised*

(Energy = strength to do things, liveliness)

By now Jak Mac Peat had many favourite pursuits which made up his day and from the moment he opened his eyes, he was involved in a hive of activity, generously interspersed with naps of varying lengths throughout the day. Dogs live in the moment and Jak's every moment was full of something.

Watching TV was an occasional pleasure. As we didn't own an HD TV, he had to make do with watching an ordinary one but apparently (unlike the USA) there are enough lines down the screen for him to watch the pictures of Animal Planet quite clearly and from time to time he would do that.

Dogs are very sociable animals and enjoy the company of other dogs. Unfortunately at that time, Jak's social circle consisted only of his daily activity of watching the Doberman (who lived across the road,) pass the window twice a day, plus a few stuffed toys from the market! Occasionally, he would change his friends and make a fresh selection from his toy box.

Sitting on the back step, nose in the air catching the smells floating past was another exciting activity. As were squeaky toys, the extending dog lead, the word 'walkies' and the wonderful aroma of 'cheeeeeeese.' All provided an amazing energy to even the most tired little dog.

Best of all was when visitors came round. The signs that visitors were a distinct possibility were always there prior to the visit: all toys put away, a vigorous rubbing of furniture with a yellow duster, followed by an obsessive hoovering of carpets and all this usually ending with a hive of activity in the kitchen. Visitors usually meant one of two things – an evening of either pure bliss, being petted constantly or if the urge overcame him too strongly to join in the festivities, then that usually led to an evening in the back kitchen merely listening to the fun in the rest of the house. Never mind, who knows what tomorrow may bring?

****

God has made us body, soul and spirit. He wants us to be whole healthy people and it is important that you have times of leisure, doing things which you love to do. Whenever you do something which drains you, make sure you include something enjoyable in your life. If you are involved with people who drain you, speak to or meet with people who motivate and inspire you too. Keep your emotional energy topped up high. Don't let it drain down.

Question:

List the things that give you energy. What do you love to do? List some things you enjoy doing. When did you last include these in your day?

Prayer:

Thank God that He has made you body, soul and spirit and He wants you to be strengthened in every way for His glory.

Meditation:

Psalm 138:3 *In the day when I cried out, you answered me, and made me bold with strength in my soul.*

Other:

None

Further study:

Now select more Bible verses which speak about how you will be energised as you follow God.

Notes:

8

You are *Nourished*

*(Nourish = keep a person, animal or plant
alive and well by means of food)*

Jak Mac Peat was quickly becoming part of our world and the
household was now re-organised, with his sleeping place upstairs,
his pooing place in the garden and his toy box in the kitchen
(although he always kept his best bones and his squeakiest toys
under the settee!)

Up until Jak arrived in our home, I thought dogs ate everything
which was placed in front of them. At least our last two dogs did.
But Jak's feeding habit was a different matter. He just didn't eat!
Or he didn't want to eat the right things. Chocolate, cheese, liver
and all the things that are off menu or to be served sparingly, he
seemed to love but if at any time these were forbidden, he wasn't
going to eat anything at all.

After failing at the tried and tested method of putting the food
down for ten minutes and then removing it until the next meal
time, I resorted to sprinkling tiny bits of grated cheese over the dog

meat in order to encourage participation in meal times. It would certainly keep him busy for a while but only in meticulously picking out all the bits of grated cheese and leaving the rest.

On one occasion, I put some nice dried food into a treat ball (which for the uninitiated is a hollow ball with a hole in, which is filled with food. The dog rolls the ball round, the food drops out and the dog eats it...easy really). When I returned home, I found the whole floor was covered with the dog meal as Jak had emptied the ball, picked out the things he liked and left the rest.

Knowing that our interaction with dogs affect their taste buds, I tried many things in order to assist his dietary habits including: jumping up and down in excitement at the arrival of the food bowl, pretending to eat the contents myself, running round the room with it and lastly, even opening the dog's mouth and pushing it in! But it was obvious that unlike many dogs, obesity would never be the number one problem of our dog. We tried starving him, coaxing him, exhausting him and bribing him but still nothing encouraged him to eat more than a few crumbs of whatever we had prepared. Someone told me that they eat more in the presence of another dog. "Maybe I should rent another dog for meal times?" I thought. But surely, that was a bit extreme? The twenty-eight teeth that he had developed by four weeks of age were not going to be in great demand, that was for sure!

Eventually, on persevering with every type of dog food known to man, on the advice of the vet, he graduated to chicken! Game, set and match to Jak Mac Peat! And so, he is nourished by chicken (and with some reluctance on his part, rice and pasta too). Serve anything else and we still find it two weeks later buried in the bed or down the sofa!

****

God has provided things in order to keep us well nourished. But how many times do we hear of people, when under stress, taking 'time out' from church and other Christian pursuits when that is the very time they need 'time in'? How strange that whenever we have a few moments with God, in prayer or reading the word, the phone rings, the text arrives, the e-mail pings? Could it be that there is a reason our enemy doesn't want us nourished? God provides nourishment for your spirit. Ensure you take it, every day.

Question:

How are you nourished in God? Daily? Weekly? Monthly? Is there any way you need to increase this?

Prayer:

Ask God to fill you afresh with His Holy Spirit and to feed you today.

Meditation:

Psalm 3:5 *I lay down and slept; I awoke for the Lord sustained me.*

Other:

Psalm 23:5, 81:16

Further study:

Now select more Bible verses which assure you of ways of being nourished in God.

Notes:

9

You are *Enlightened*

(Enlighten = give knowledge to a person, inform)

There were several places which Jak disliked, and one that he disliked intensely, particularly at night time was the garden. Despite his superior vision in the dark, he would do everything he could to avoid the garden trips last thing at night.

Each evening, the routine was the same, a late evening walk and then a garden visit just prior to bedtime. He would scurry out and scurry back in, but I could always see his frightened eyes shining green in the dark.

At the bottom of the garden beyond the fence lived two alsatians. They were outdoor dogs but rarely were they peering through the fence at night. Usually they were snuggled down, tucked up in their garden kennel, away from the harshness of the Scottish night. Those rooks with their huge beaks, (who frequented his daytime garden trips by sitting on the fence, calling to each other as Jak eyed them nervously), were sleeping in their rookery high in the trees next to the house.

Maybe it was something he could see? I wondered if his nervous glances towards the bushes gave us a clue of the problem? Or maybe, he was just afraid of the dark!

One day while shopping in Glasgow, I passed a large flashlight and decided to buy it. That night, Jak went out accompanied by the flashlight. I'm not sure whether it was having the light outside, as much as knowing that we were on the other end of the beam, which changed his late night visits to the garden. But the problem had gone and nowadays, sometimes it's even hard to get him in.

****

There are times we find ourselves in the dark. Periods when we need the light of God to enlighten our darkness. It is at times like these that his Word becomes a lamp to our feet and a light to our path. These are the days we walk by faith and sometimes that is hard. It is good to remind ourselves that He walks with us and to Him there is no darkness. He sees the way as clear as in the sunlight and as we walk in faith, step by step He enlightens that darkness. It is in those times He calls us to walk by faith not by sight, one step at a time until we see clearly again.

Question:

In what way has God's word enlightened your darkness in the past? Which verses/passages have been instrumental in lighting the way for you in difficult times?

Prayer:

Take some time to thank God for these 'flames in the darkness' and for what those verses revealed to you both then and now.

Meditation:

Psalm 18:28 *For you will light my lamp. The Lord my God will enlighten my darkness.*

Other:

Psalm 27:1, 36:9, 97:11, 112:4, 119:105, 119:130, 146:8

Further study:

Now choose more Bible verses which state how you are enlightened as a follower of God.

Notes:

10

You are *Trained*

*(Train = give a person instruction or practise
so that he or she becomes skilled)*

It was now time for the dog to be trained! Jak spent most of his time (when not asleep) learning new things. The border collie, the poodle and the retriever are thought to be the smartest of all dogs and although Jak was definitely not in their league, we were doing our very best to train him.

With a puppy, the blackboard of their mind is empty so learning is fast. Life can be confusing at times but slowly, he was grasping the basic facts of life. He had already acquired quite a few new concepts such as:

1. Balls roll downhill, not uphill.

2. Your tail is always behind you, ready to chase at a moment's notice.

3. The resident cat is a great means of exercise whenever and wherever you can find him.

4. The costume you were born with fits much better than a home knitted sweater, antlers or bootees!

5. When a human bares their teeth, it means they like me!

There are also important questions to be answered such as:

* When learning to use a lead, is what I want to get to, worth not being able to breathe?

* Is the reward offered to stop 'sinning' worth more than the pleasure of the sin?

* If I stand here long enough, will someone eventually notice and that treat jar get opened?

* Is the fun of chasing the cat, worth the pain of the result?

Puppies learn 'bite inhibition' from their siblings. When a puppy bites his siblings, the victim squeals and retaliation occurs. But Jak had no siblings now. His only pack members were us and the cat. A few yells and ouches from us (that is Kevin and myself) following each puppy nip seemed to help a little but without doubt one bash round the nose from the cat cured the situation overnight. It was quite clear who was really the pack leader in our house!

****

From the moment we joined His family, God began our training. It was on that day that we entered His classroom and began our lessons. Sometimes it seems that there are no answers to the questions on the chalkboard of life. As difficult situations come our way, we have no idea when break time will arrive or when the end of the day will be for this particular issue. There is no clock on the wall to mark our progress through the situation.

But there are things of which we can be sure: that all things work together for good, that He trains our hands for war and our fingers for battle and that nothing is ever wasted. Our God is in control.

Question:

What has been your biggest lesson in life and what did you learn?

Prayer:

Thank Him that He was/is with you during that time and for each of the things He taught/teaches you through it.

Meditation:

Psalm 144:1 *Blessed be the Lord my rock, who trains my hands for war and my fingers for battle.*

Further study:

You are *Growing:* Psalm 92:12-14

You are *Taught:* Psalm 18:34, 25:8-9, 25:12, 32:8, 94:12

You are *Moulded*: Psalm 33:15

Notes:

11

You are *An Heir*

(Inherit = receive money, property or title etc
when the previous owner dies)

When Jak left his doggie pack, he didn't know that he would never have another one. At least not an animal one. But when we adopted him, he became part of our pack.

On his arrival, he inherited the things vital to any self respecting dog – and then over the next few weeks a basket, a ball, a blanket with paws on, a blue octopus, a blue rain mac and an ever increasing set of squeaky toys.

And Jak, as with most dogs, was a natural social climber, always on the look out for signs of weakness, ready to assert himself at any sign of lack of self confidence in the higher pack members.

He knew the pack rules well. He understood that pack members should walk together and at the twitch of a lead, was instantly lined up at the door with duffle bag and pac a mac at the ready! He knew that a pack should nap together and after tea along with his master, he could usually be found in a sleepy heap, paws pounding as he no doubt pursued some 'runaway Jaffa Cake over the Himalayan mountains'. He knew that a pack should eat together (this was a hard one) and they should sleep together too. He had this last art perfected. Many mornings, Kevin and I awoke to find ourselves teetering on either edge of the bed, with the dog stretched out horizontally across the centre, front and back paws extended to fullest extent!

I read somewhere that 33% of dog owners talk to their dogs on the phone, 58% include them in on family photos and 70% sign their name on birthday and Christmas cards! We were no exception to a couple of those things I must admit!

As with most dogs, he was in fact an heir to not only a lot of doggy possessions but also loads of love and cuddles and everything that goes along with being part of a family.

******

You and I, on the day we gave our lives to God, became heirs of God. Adopted into His family, we are no longer on the outside, and able to inherit all that entails. I often wonder, do I really fully partake in all He offers me? When I go to meet Him, will there be a pile of unused things which were prepared for me to use on this earth? Will I hear those words, "It could have been so much easier had you partaken of all I had given for you to use on earth?" I hope not. I do hope that the supplies He has for me are well used, right up to that day when I meet Him face to face to begin to enjoy my biggest inheritance ever.

Question:

When you became a Christian, what things did you become an heir to?

Prayer:

Now take time to thank Him that He adopted you into His family and for all that you have inherited as a result.

Meditation:

Psalm 37:29 *The righteous shall inherit the land and dwell in it forever.*

Other:

Psalm 37:22

Further study:

Now choose more Bible verses which state what you inherit as a follower of God.

Notes:

12

You are *Delivered*

(Deliver = rescue, set free)

It was going to be a beautiful day. The signs were in the sky. I rose at 8am, dressed quickly and took the lead down from the shelf. Jak emerged from somewhere under the bedcovers and in an instant was first in the queue by the door.

When we are staying in our flat in England, having no garden, we are always fairly prompt for the first walk of the day and very soon we were descending the two flights of stairs, and emerging into the clear morning air.

One of my favourite things in life is coming out onto the seafront and seeing the amazing ocean before me. The second best thing, on the rare occasions I get to do it, is walking alongside it at the start of the day. And so that's what we did.

Walking along the seafront was beautiful that day so on reaching the end of the promenade, I decided to make my way down onto the sand. Once there, it was evident that the receding tide had deposited a whole layer of large stones and pebbles across the upper part of the beach which I needed to cross in order to reach the sea. Nevertheless, I decided to continue onwards...dragging a very unenthusiastic dog with me. Finding the largest stones up to his chest, Jak reached the middle of the mass, slipping and sliding around and then just came to a halt. I wandered on towards the sea, and after a while looked back. Jak was still standing stationary with his most pathetic face displayed and definitely not going anywhere!

I went further towards the sea, thinking that he didn't like to be far from me and he would follow. I stopped and beckoned to the tiny dog in the middle of the uneven ground. No movement. Calling, shouting, beckoning, jumping up and down... nothing would persuade him to move.

Eventually, I made my way back and looking down, realised that every stone was like a mini mountain to him and every space between them, like a mini chasm.

I reached down and lifted the little dog high above the stones and walked on towards the sea.

****

Our God is a deliverer! Not only on that day you made a commitment to Him, did He deliver you from the things you justly deserve. Not only has He delivered you from the implications of whatever life you would have chosen, if you had not made that choice. He also continues to deliver you daily, out of many situations you would find yourself in. Of some things, you will be aware but I am sure that of some, you have no idea that He has stepped in and moved in your situation. Moment by moment, right though your life, and then as you enter eternity, He is indeed your deliverer.

Question:

How has God delivered you from circumstances, throughout your life? Has He caused you to walk through them or has He removed them? Give examples.

Prayer:

Thank Him for that deliverance and ask Him to increase His hand upon you today.

Meditation:

Psalm 18:19 *He also brought me out into a broad place; He delivered me because He delighted in me.*

Other:

Psalm 18:43, 18:48, 33:18-19, 34:4, 34:7, 34:19, 34:17, 37:40, 40:17, 41:1, 50:15, 54:7, 91:3, 91:14-15, 97:10, 107:6, 107:13, 107:28

Further study:

You are *Saved:* Psalm 34:6, 34:18, 91:16, 109:30-31, 116:6, 118:14, 118:21, 138:7, 149:4

Notes:

13

You are *Healed*

(Heal = make or become healthy flesh again)

From time to time, it becomes the challenge of every dog owner to give their dog a pill. We were no different and one particular day we arrived home from the vet's with a little white box of pills. "Give dog one pill three times a day" said the instructions. "Easy" we thought, not for a minute understanding the incredible depth in that word 'give'.

Right from the start it was obvious to us that our puppy had done an in-depth study of the manual 'How to know if your piece of cheese has a pill inside'. Maybe it was prophetic insight but somehow he knew! And when we hid a pill in his food, he certainly seemed to have a degree in 'pill extraction'. Occasionally we triumphed and he tucked into a tasty piece of chicken and got a nasty surprise but more often, we would carefully conceal a pill in a morsel of food and then watch with baited breath as he began to eat, only to witness a little white pill left on an empty plate, when everything else had been eaten.

I have to admit on some occasions, we took the law into our own hands and carefully securing all four legs, neatly dropped the pill onto the back of his tongue and rubbed his throat vigorously. But even then, you could almost guarantee that after sitting with the dog for five minutes to make sure it had gone, we would later find the pill somewhere else in the room! How does that happen? At least you would think he would have the sense to hide it!

****

God is healing you. Whether physically, mentally, emotionally or spiritually, He wants to increase the health you have at this moment and bring you healing. Sometimes He allows us to walk through things that we would choose not to. Why is everyone not healed? That is a question which is incredibly difficult to answer and a question which engenders endless debate. Nevertheless, He is a father who loves you and is with you in your suffering. Whatever way He chooses to heal you, emotionally, physically or however...and wherever you are in that process, allow it to bring you closer to Him.

Question:

Have you ever been healed in any of the above ways? How?

Prayer:

Pray for His continued healing in your life and in the lives of those around you.

Meditation:

Psalm 147:3 *He heals the broken hearted and binds up their wounds.*

Other:

Psalm 103:3

Further study:

Now choose more Bible verses which speak about God's healing work in you.

Notes:

14

You are *Lifted*

(Lift = raise, pick up)

We had recently revised the rules for night time and decreed that Jak should spend his night *on* the bed, not *in* the bed. The reason for this, being that the situation was getting very close to us having to ask permission to be under the covers with the dog! Having had to re-establish that decree several times during one particular night, morning came and we all got up. But one of us was not a happy doggy.

The morning continued to go downhill when the refuse collector arrived, followed by the window cleaner. Convinced each week that some men are stealing our stuff, at the sight of the bin lorry Jak usually runs from room to room, frantic to save the empty bean tins, mouldy bread and everything else that pours from our bin into the big lorry.

On this occasion, on frightening away the wicked men with the lorry, he was then faced with three more, equipped with ladders, who proceeded to climb to the upper windows in an attempt to 'who knows what?' That seemed to make it very necessary not only to race across the lounge from chair to chair but also to race around the house from room to room and floor to floor.

Suddenly, the divine quest of 'Superdog' seemed to be to prevent at any cost the entrance into the house by three men with ladders, buckets of water and chamois leathers! The stairway became a ski slope and the rooms a race track. As the men heeded the warning, and after trying to enter at the upstairs windows, began to descend their ladders, all was going well. But Jak was in fine form, running faster and faster…that was until the speed of his body became faster than his legs and he tumbled from the top to the bottom of the stairs in a ball of flying fur and the Ferrari-dog suddenly became a tangled mess deposited on the welcome mat at the bottom.

Hearing the clatter, I rushed down the stairs and picked him up. I lifted him high into the air. He was yelling in a way that injured dogs do and his leg was sticking out in a really odd way. To cut a very long story short, after ten minutes of squealing, thirty minutes of trembling (and two weeks of refusing to go near the stairs), all was well that ended well. The men with the ladders went away, the bin men didn't come back for a week and that night of course, he was back under the covers!

****

God wants to lift you up. When man lifts you, it is only to the limit of his reach but when God lifts you it is as far as you dare to think, hope, dream or imagine. He wants you to fly. He wants to give you accelerated speed in everyday life. When you enter the flow of the wind of the spirit for your life, that wind can take you to places you have never dreamed of. He can propel you forward, He can open doors, He can make a way where there is no way. The key is to enter into the flow of what He wants to do for you and the effects become limitless.

Question:

Are you in the flow of the wind of the spirit for your life right now? Why do you answer as you do?

Prayer:

Ask God today to let His wind blow afresh on you in every way right now and give Him permission to allow that breath of God to blow on others, through your life this week.

Meditation:

Psalm 117:7-8 *He raises the poor out of the dust, and lifts the needy out of the ash heap, that he may sit him with princes – with the princes of his people.*

Other:

Psalm 18:33, 18:35, 37:24, 27:5-6, 40:2, 113:7-8, 119:117, 145:14, 146:8-9, 147:6

Further study:

You are *Upheld:* Psalm 37:24, 37:17, 41:12, 119:116

Notes:

15

You are
Watched Over

*(Watch = look at a person or thing for some time; be on
guard or ready for something to happen; take care of something)*

Apart from a regular attempt to feign lameness in order to gain
attention, Jak seemed none the worse for his nasty experience on
the stairs. He had always been a clingy puppy and used to, and still
does, follow us from room to room. Even when enjoying his best
dream such as the eventual defeat of the alsatians through the
fence, he still has one eye on us whenever we rise to leave the
room.

Apparently a pup's earliest experiences have a tremendous impact
on his adult mind. Stresses are not bad, in fact the mother creates
some stresses specifically designed to help bring about
independence.

From the age of four or five weeks, the nursing mother will begin
to walk away as the pup tries to nurse and the relationship changes
from one of care/dependency to dominance/submission. This stage

is very necessary to the newborn, and in fact pups which are raised under non punishing conditions are sometimes very difficult to train.

Once transferred to a human pack leader, any injuries, fears or loneliness that are healed with affection and attention from that person, tend to produce a very strong bond.

Nevertheless, Jak was gradually growing in confidence in every place except the garden. At first it was just a night time problem but as time went by, his dislike of the garden grew to twenty-four hours a day.

There were *some* things he liked about the garden. He used it as a storage centre for old socks or stolen underwear or any other treasure raided from the house. It made a great rolling arena when a dead bird made our garden its final resting place. The garden was a wonderful area too for eating fox poo. In fact there were a whole lot of reasons that he really liked the garden.

But stay alone, he would *not*. Each and every ten seconds, whatever he was doing or wherever he was, he would glance back to the door to check I was still there. If for a second, I left the patio door to tend to the cooker or to switch on the kettle, he was inside, in an instant. Outdoors was a big adventure only as long as someone was watching over him!

****

The Bible clearly tells us several times that our Father in Heaven watches over our lives. He considers all we do. When we are

66

happy, excited, motivated and on top of the world, He is watching us. When we are sad, grieving, tired, depressed or anxious, He is watching us. Wherever you are, He is watching you and He is with you right now.

Question:

In what circumstances just now, do you need to feel that God is present watching over you?

Prayer:

Invite Him afresh to be with you in those situations today.

Meditation:

Psalm 33:15 *He fashions their hearts individually; He considers all their works.*

Other:

Psalm 16:8, 33:18, 34:15, 40:17, 41:12, 53:2, 102:19, 139:2-3, 142:3, 146:9

Further study:

You are *Understood:* Psalm 139 2

Notes:

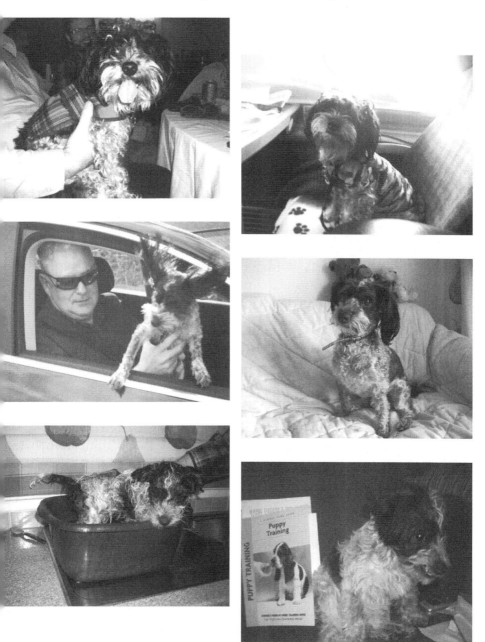

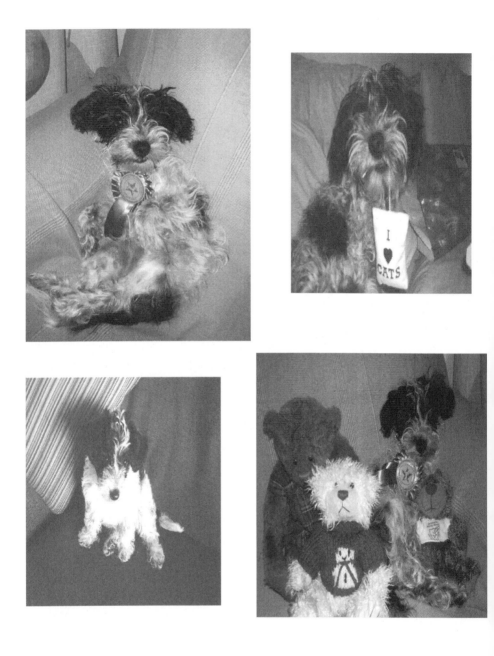

16

You are *Guided*

(Guide = a person who shows others the way or
points out interesting sights; To guide = act as a guide to)

A dog has an amazing sense of smell. He is born blind and deaf but along with his sense of taste, his ability to smell is alive and well right from the first moment of life and there are millions of scents that pass his nose on any given day.

He is able to differentiate between thousands of different odours and if a pot of stew were cooking on the stove, a human would smell the stew but the dog would smell the beef, carrots, potatoes, peas, spices and all the other individual ingredients. He has two hundred and twenty million scent receptors in order to do this and if you laid out the membranes inside his nose, they would be larger than the dog himself.

A dog is able to detect and identify people and things by their scent and his smell memories last for a lifetime. Scent is in fact one of the major means of communication for a dog. That's why when dogs go out, they leave little packets of information on the lampposts for others to find! When the next dog comes past, it knows his sex, his state of health, if he's nervous or stressed and how long it's been since he marked this particular bit of territory.

It never fails to amaze me that when we go to a hotel room, Jak only needs to go once, then out of a corridor full of doors, he knows which one is our door. How amazing is that? He is guided by his sense of smell.

****

God wants to guide each step of our lives and in order to do that, He gives us signposts as guidance along the way. The Word of God, sermons, advice, prophetic insight, dreams and almost anything can provide us with His guidance and direction for our lives once we are tuned in to His voice. He wants to guide your life. Every day of it.

Question:

Think of the big decisions you have made. Have you checked His guidance? If so, how did He guide you?

Prayer:

Thank Him for His guidance in your life and reaffirm your willingness to hear His voice each day and follow his direction.

Meditation:

Psalm 32 8: *I will instruct you and teach you in the way you should go: I will guide you with my eye.*

Other:

Psalm 18:36, 25:9, 31:3, 37:23, 78:72, 139:9-10

Further study:

You are *Led:* Psalm 23:2-3, 31:8, 143:10

Notes:

17

You are *Given Joy*

(Joy = a feeling of great pleasure; gladness)

It never failed to amuse me each time we moved between our base in North West England and our home in Scotland, how pleased the dog was to see his toys! One would think between visits, a dog would forget the blue octopus, the hide chew stick or the rubber rabbit he holds dear but no, each time the little dog arrived at what would be his home for the next few days, he embarked on a hot pursuit to search out the few toys he had left behind, and showed incredible joy to see each one of them!

It still makes me smile to see him head first in the dog toy box, front paws in too, digging away pulling out toy after toy until, finding the very one he wants he waddles away leaving rejected toys all over the kitchen floor. I wonder, does he know which one he is looking for before he starts or does he make his selection once he gets tired of digging?

When acquiring a new addition to his precious toy collection he will race round, shake it, toss it into the air again and again and run to fetch it and toss it again showing absolute delight in his new acquisition.

Most dogs like to play. Play does many things for an animal. Play helps dogs develop communal behaviour, it develops coordination and apparently it teaches problem solving too (maybe we should all play more!) It develops the mind, enhances their experience of life and does a whole host of other things but for Jak it does nothing greater than bring him joy.

****

The Bible says the joy of the Lord is our strength. And joy in our life has an incredible effect on us physically, mentally, emotionally and spiritually. Every time we laugh a whole host of things happen to us. The benefits to us physically, mentally, emotionally and spiritually are amazing and something that doctors are now discovering, God has been telling us for thousands of years. His deep joy can be fully resident in our daily experience whatever the circumstances and fill our life with the many benefits that brings.

Question:

What gives you joy? Is there a way you can incorporate more of this into your life?

Prayer:

Thank God for all the things which bring you joy in this life. Now talk to Him about the unsurpassable joy you will experience beyond this life which will be greater than the best moment you have ever experienced on earth.

Meditation:

Psalm 16:11 *You will show me the path of life; In your presence is fullness of joy; At your right hand are pleasures forevermore.*

Other:

Psalm 21:6, 30:11-12, 97:11, 144:15

Further study:

Now select more Bible verses which give the promise of joy to you.

Notes:

18

You are *Spoken To*

(Spoken to = say something in order to convey information or to express a feeling; talk to in order to reprove or advise)

Asleep on the floor, Jak's chest moved up and down as he enjoyed a late afternoon sleep in the sun. Watching him, I noticed his breathing stop, his eyes flicker as he began in hot pursuit of a 'sausage across a motorway' or something similar in his doggy dreams.

Suddenly, he sat up, dream interrupted and listened. His head cocked from side to side and his ears rotated in a strange fashion as he listened intently. I listened and heard nothing. Within a second, he was at the window peering out into the evening. I looked out myself into the driveway but there was nothing but my own car, parked outside the window. Attempting to command him down from the window and telling him his master would be another hour or so returning home, did not deter his vigil.

A dog's hearing is superior to ours. They can hear from four times the distance than us, four times as loud, and hear frequencies much higher and lower than a human ear. Their ears move to scan as they listen and they can distinguish many different nuances of sound. The eighteen or so muscles which tilt, rotate, raise and lower their ears ensure they identify the location of the sound much quicker than us. They hear the heartbeat of a rabbit and the tiny squeak of a mouse. They are able to discern the different footsteps of their owner, the postman and neighbour and are incredibly sensitive to voice pitch, tone and word pronunciation. They can discern between the engine of their master's car and that of their neighbour's.

Jak continued to sit at the window for a couple more minutes after which amazingly, Kevin's car arrived in the driveway, unexpectedly at least one hour early. How did he know? He could hear because he was listening and was sensitive to his master's arrival.

****

God calls us into the secret place with Him where we can hear His slightest whispers. He speaks in the earthquake, wind and fire but sometimes He uses just a still small voice. Sometimes He calls us past the outer court, past the inner court and into the Holy of Holies where He can whisper His words and we know His awesome presence. And sometimes there is no need for words but in the stillness we find His company is all we need.

Question:

Are there times you have spent with God in that secret place where there are no need for words? When were those times?

Prayer:

Find a quiet place and enjoy His presence in the silence today.

Meditation:

Psalm 85:8 *I will hear what God the Lord will speak, for He will speak peace to His people and to His saints.*

Other:

Psalm 40:6

Further study:

You are *Sung Over:* Psalm 42:8

Notes:

19

You are *Given Health*

(Health = the condition of a person's body or mind)

Right from the start we aimed to make our little dog fit and healthy. With several walks a day, the correct amount of quality puppy food and not too many treats, we felt that things were coming together pretty well.

We knew the rule: 'Don't feed him from your plate or he'll soon expect a place at the table' and so he owned his own cream coloured food bowl in the shape of a dog and a water bowl with a fish on (actually donated by the cat). The second reason for the personalised crockery set was that we didn't fancy catching one of the sixty five diseases that can be passed onto humans from our much loved canine companions.

Life was progressing pretty well with his health and safety regime until the day came to go to the V....... E........T.......! He seemed to enjoy the journey as he thought we were going to the park but was definitely puzzled when we pulled into the car park of a big white house which was completely new territory to Jak.

We sat for a moment and he stared at the array of dogs, cats, birds and rabbits which were making their way into the big white house, accompanied by their owners. By the wag of his tail, he obviously thought we were going to a party! He even looked quite eager as we left the car and followed the procession. That was until we got inside the white building. He then found himself surrounded by the same collection of animals, most of whom now looked distinctly worried and there wasn't a party hat to be seen anywhere! He looked even more concerned when one owner took a dog into a little room and came back out without him!

I suppose when you consider it, the next few events were not the most comfortable ones of his life...being taken into a room to stand in front of a stranger dressed up in a white coat, being made to stand on a table in the middle of the room (which is strictly forbidden at home) and having instruments inserted into every and any unguarded orifice he possessed! The experience progressed towards having a thermometer stuck up his bottom and a needle stuck in his neck and the grand finale consisted of having his anal glands expressed!

Hardly surprising the next time we got into the car, he didn't want to come!

****

Following God is a healthy thing to do! Not that it guarantees a life free of sickness but the effects of living for Him have got to be good. Think about it. Physically we are, or become free from harmful substances such as excessive drink, drugs or nicotine. Emotionally we are part of a healthy social circle in our fellowship, have closer relationships, have opportunity for counselling and are able at any time to pour out our anxieties to the Lord in prayer. Mentally we are committed to lifelong learning in bible study and regularly receiving teaching in church. Spiritually we are alive and growing the whole of our lives and can be more alive at the end than at the start. There is no ageism in the things of the Spirit.

Question:

Is your Christian life adding the good things listed above to your life? What is missing?

Prayer:

Pray that God will bless your health, wherever you are in your journey of life. Pray for others too in this area.

Meditation:

Psalm 92:13-14 *Those who are planted in the house of the Lord shall flourish in the courts of our God. They shall still bear fruit in old age; They shall be fresh and flourishing.*

Other:

Psalm 103:5

Further study:

Now select more Bible verses which promise health in some way to you.

Notes:

20

You are *Tested*

*(Tested = take measures to check the quality,
performance or reliability of something, especially
before putting it into widespread use)*

As one year in doggie terms is said to equal seven in human years, I decided that at two years of age, Jak was definitely a teenager. It's not easy to take a teenager to the hairdressers and it's even worse taking an adolescent dog to the doggy parlour!

We arrived at Pampered Pets, East Kilbride, for our 10.30am appointment. Jak smelt a rat as soon as we left the car and by the time we had reached the door he was positioned, stiff paws stretched out ahead of him, pulling backwards against the lead every inch of the way.

We had tried this once before when he was a small puppy, full of wide eyed wonder, open to every and any opportunity to experience life in all it's fullness! This time, he knew where he was headed and was definitely not a happy chappy. Once through the door, he took up residence in the far corner of the small waiting area, pressing himself into the wall as though he had only minutes to live. I must admit that as I passed him over to the 'nice lady' I didn't envy him, but I envied their job a lot less.

Two hours later I returned to a 'look' in both his, and their eyes that said...never again! The bath had been fairly uneventful but the clipping had ended with him climbing up round the neck of the 'clippist' (is that the right word? I don't think so) in a scarf like fashion, and her having to be rescued by two more of the team because he wouldn't come down! When I returned to Pampered Pets he was standing on a table (another table!) with three people sitting around him, one holding his body, another his legs and the last doing the dirty deed. We went for total humiliation that day and ended with a puff of perfume!

As he, eyes bulging, dragged me clutching the end of the lead, toward the door, I couldn't help giving a glance at the neatly lined up rows of dogs, patiently waiting in cages, or on tables or in large sinks, to be attended to. 'Why can't my dog be like that?' I thought.

Bit of a test today, difficult and scary at times but at least we're through it. For this time anyway!

****

Have you ever been through a time of testing? I would guess if you've been on the road any length of time, then the answer is most definitely 'yes'. As a teacher, I know that tests monitor progress made and they direct future learning. They highlight specific weak areas and they give a comparison with others on the same learning journey. In life, we think of a test as uncomfortable. God sees tests as necessary to our learning and our progress. But one thing is sure, He will not test us more than we are able to take. That is His promise.

Question:

Identify in your mind a recent test of your own...how was God testing you? Did you pass or fail the test?

Prayer:

Thank Him that He has provided a way through, not only that test, but everything else that may cross your path.

Meditation:

Psalm 11:5 *The Lord tests the righteous, but the wicked and the one who loves violence his soul hates.*

Other:

Psalm 7:9

Further study:

Now select more Bible verses which state how you are calmed as a follower of God.

Notes:

21

You are *Given Victory*

*(Victory = success won against an
opponent in a battle, contest or game)*

Jak was very definitely part of a human world. Our life consisted of travelling between Scotland, England and Wales, many church meetings and a lot of socialising. It didn't include a great amount of pet shop visits, veterinary surgery tours or zoos! Therefore, as Jak was with us the majority of the time, his exposure to animals was limited. I suppose he did see my elephant slippers every morning, which would be some experience should he ever have to fight a real live elephant in Glasgow!

That was until that very first time he met the two alsatians who lived the other side of our garden fence. "Having a wooden fence with spaces through to the neighbour's garden will be interesting," I thought as I watched the dogs gaze through the slats.

When he initially arrived, the alsatians spent a lot of their time staring through the fence into our garden at Jak, who they definitely perceived as some sort of oddity and probably not a dog at all. They watched one day intrigued, as he balanced his front paws on a football, walking around on his back legs. They stared quizzically, heads on one side and then the other, as the little dog carried his huge hoop around the lawn.

One day, Jak noticed the two huge dogs staring through the fence. Immediately, he marched up to the fence and barked right in their faces. The two astonished dogs backed off and disappeared further back on the lawn. This became a regular routine and Jak soon became registered as the pack leader, at least in his mind. Day by day even now, he will creep closer and closer and when one inch away, bark right in their faces. Little does he realise that without the fence he would be a distant memory of a dog in thirty seconds flat! The victory isn't Jak's. The victory belongs to the fence!

****

I wonder, how many times is God the invisible fence around us? How many times is He there with a protection, of which we have no idea? I'm sure there are many times we feel the victory is ours and we have no idea how or when God intervened. May He continue to be our invisible fence every day of our lives.

Question:

Are there any examples in your experience when you know it has seemed like the victory was yours but God was involved?

Prayer:

Thank Him for the times He has fenced you in and for the fact that He wants to do that. Pray for whoever you feel needs that protection at this time.

Meditation:

Psalm 118:6 *The Lord is on my side; I will not fear. What can man do to me?*

Other:

Psalm 118:11, 118:16

Further study:

Now choose more Bible verses which state that you are given victory as a follower of God.

Notes:

22

You are *Satisfied*

(Satisfy = give a person what is needed or wanted)

"Does he have anything to worry about?" asked the vet. "I don't think so..." I replied, my compulsive anthropomorphizing imagination picturing him sitting at home biting his nails. "He's got a stomach ulcer," he continued.

And so with instructions to watch out for tell tale sights of stress, give him a settled care filled routine and clutching a packet of fourteen very expensive tablets, Jak and I left the building. "Drama queen," I muttered to the dog as we crossed the car park and set out for home.

There are certain things in a dog's life which are basic needs in order that he will thrive and become a fully balanced member of the dog family. I checked them off in my mind as we travelled home.

Clean water? Hmmm – dog prefers milk, horlicks or tea with two sugars!

A balanced diet of good dog food? ...have tried every dog food known to man and still he will not eat it. Have tried coaxing, rewarding, ignoring, removing, force feeding and eating it myself. Have now compromised with chicken, rice and pasta!

Shelter and safety? More or less satisfactory I think.

Physical care such as walks (oh yeeeees!) and vet visits (oh noooooo!)

Nurture and play? We are working on this one. Dog prefers to throw things by picking them up, shaking his head and then letting them go. I fetch them back and hand them to him. Process starts over again. He throws and we fetch! Something's wrong somewhere...

Its own space? Own space not greatly used. As mentioned before, dog prefers a horizontal position, nose and tail extended to maximum length across centre of bed with us perched on either end!

Bathing, grooming etc? Grooming definitely still a game. One brush, one grab, pull brush away, dog tries to get hold of brush, when dog looking the other way brush again, dog jumps round to grab. Wave brush about to extricate dog's teeth from brush, third grab, tug of war with dog using brush as rope. I suppose it does seem a bit of a game really!

Training, discipline and boundaries? Ho ho ho...(though we are working on it!)

A pack, company and a bond with humans? No problem here, our dog resembles a leech most of the time and where we go, it goes too!

Satisfied that we ticked off most of the requirements, we arrived home and set off on the second adventure of the day...giving him his tablet!

****

There are many things I enjoy which are secular. Classical concerts, shopping, the seaside, walking in the country are all immensely satisfying. And yet, in each one of us there is a God shaped space which nothing else can satisfy. As fulfilling as all these things may be, there is nothing in the world which satisfies like a touch from God Himself and experiencing His presence. He brings us a satisfaction that nothing and no one else can.

Question:

What was your most powerful experience of God? Think back to that time. Or do you need to ask God to begin to touch your life today…either again, or for the first time?

Prayer:

Thank Him for the depth of His presence and begin a new journey today, to search that out once again. Talk to God about where you are in that journey of knowing His touch.

Meditation:

Psalm 107:9 *For He satisfies the longing soul, and fills the hungry soul with goodness.*

Other:

Psalm 63:5, 65:4, 91:16, 103:5

Further study:

You are *Fulfilled*: Psalm 21:2, 145:19

Notes:

23

You are *Given Peace*

(Peace = freedom from disturbance; tranquillity)

It is a considered fact that dogs dream and as they do, it is thought that their brains experience the same electrical activity observed in humans. Often when asleep, Jak would be quivering, whimpering, running in the air and growling as he chased a 'giant kitten dressed as a tree' or entered into some other obscure dream or other. I wonder if he knew that his ear deafening growl was a mere whimper and his leap across the chasm was a paw-twitch on the carpet?

I read somewhere that a puppy's growth hormone is not fully released until it is asleep and it was obvious to all from day one that Jak was fully committed to getting as big as he could!

Back when he was a tiny puppy on one occasion, I needed to travel from Glasgow to the south part of England. Armed with puppy food, blanket with paws on, dog treats, emergency water, wee mats, a dog basket, food and water bowls, dog carrier, poo bags and two toys, I set off on the journey. I was not sure how he would react to the car.

I suppose it must be quite strange after much walking past the 'very large light blue box' on the driveway, to one day discover there's a door in the side and be expected to get in it! You discover there's a little room inside with seats all facing the same way and windows to look out at the bird table in the garden! No doubt it becomes scarier still when the owner shuts the door and you're in there all alone. But that is nothing to when they get in this room beside you, there's a rumbling sound and the room starts to shake and then move slowly off the drive! And before long you are whizzing at 70mph down the M74 towards Carlisle, which is full of other little boxes of various colours all doing the same. Every one has people in them and there's even one or two with dogs in them too! I'm sure that car travel must be an interesting experience if you're a puppy!

Nevertheless I set off with Jak, in new dog harness fastened to the front seat, stretching his neck trying to look at the cars passing us by. We drove to the end of the road, turned right and then right again onto the main road to begin our journey. We had travelled for five minutes and interested to see my dog's reaction to this new experience, I looked down to view him fast asleep and very soon flat on his back, paws in the air. Out of our six hundred mile return journey, he must have slept five hundred and ninety of them, oblivious to the dangers of the roads and the responsibility of safety, totally at peace in the knowledge that someone was in control.

****

Life happens between our ears! It's not the events which affect how we feel, it's how we respond to those events. God has promised us a peace which passes understanding. He has let us know it's available for the taking. That means it's a peace which sometimes doesn't make sense, a peace we have in the midst of events which are anything but peaceful. Consequently, if we can find this peace on the inside then it doesn't matter to us so much what happens on the outside. So often we experience the worries but the event never 'happens'. Jesus has planned it the other way round, that when we do have a 'happening' we don't have the worry. It's finding that place that's the thing...

Question:

What worries have you had that have 'never happened?' What happenings have you had and you've 'never worried'?

Prayer:

Pray that God will give you the ability to avoid the first and to do the second, more and more.

Meditation:

Psalm 37:11 *But the meek shall inherit the earth, and shall delight themselves in the abundance of peace.*

Other:

Psalm 37:7, 85:8, 147:14

Further study:

Now select more Bible verses which promise peace in some way to you.

Notes:

24

You are *Drawn Close*

(Close = near)

After the six hundred mile round trip Jak soon got used to being in the big tin box with wheels, and used to enjoy the passing scenery of the street as we drove various places.

A favourite trip was to one of the seventy plus parks in Glasgow. One day we pulled up in Strathclyde Park, Motherwell. He seemed to find the scents exhilarating. The experts say it's similar to you and I stepping out of the house and the sky being a brilliant blue and the grass a dazzling emerald green and each and every colour brilliant and beautiful to the eyes. They think that's what happens to dogs when they go to a place full of new scents to smell. That's what it looked like with Jak anyway.

In fact it was on that park that he performed his brand new trick for the first time, that of sitting his bottom on the floor, lifting his back legs and scooting around with his front legs, dragging his bottom behind him!

His park visit usually went as follows: head down, tail up walking in circles intent on finding just the exact spot to make use of a poo bag. A few more laps of the grass then just time for a search for a particularly nice smell to roll in, (a dead bird or a cow pat if we were in the fields), with a few fox droppings to nibble on, to end the visit off nicely. Many years ago rolling in things was apparently used in several ways. It could be as a way of carrying a message back to the pack that some animal is in the area, or sometimes as a disguise or even a way to show off a discovery to the pack back at home. Whatever he was trying to say to us, we made it clear it was not working!

Jak soon discovered that his human pack were not as impressed as his friends were by the smells he could disguise himself in. I think after a couple of occasions he felt that the gain was not worth the pain of being put in a black bag in the back of the car and once home, dropped in the dog bath and then dried off with the hair dryer.

Nevertheless whatever he did, we still picked him up and took him home. That's because he was ours!

****

The fact was, even though on occasions we wanted to tie him up to run behind the car, we didn't, we brought him close. Life is full of 'stuff' and from time to time, sometimes through our own choices and sometimes through the choices of those around us, we get touched by that stuff. But either way, when we've been out in the world there's a place close to Him where we can get cleaned down, dried off, healed and refreshed. Let Him draw you close, everyday.

Question:

What things have affected your spirit over the last day, week or month?

Prayer:

Ask God today, to draw you close, to place you under the waterfall of His Holy Spirit and clean you, heal you and refresh you. Don't talk now, just let Him do it.

Meditation:

Psalm 34:18 *The Lord is near to those who have a broken heart, and saves such as have a contrite spirit.*

Other:

Psalm 119:151, 139:5, 139:7, 140:13b, 145:18

Further study:

Now select more Bible verses which speak of how God will draw you close in times of need.

Notes:

25

You are *Set Apart*

(Apart = away from each other; separately)

In 1800 there were only fifteen specific breeds of dog. In 1900 there were more than sixty. Today there are around four hundred different breeds which come in a huge range of shapes and sizes, weights and colours.

Coats are long, short, smooth or rough, curly or straight and ears come in all shapes and sizes. Dogs are bred for their assets as the fiercest, the smallest, the fastest, the cuddliest the best sniffer or retriever or shepherd. No other animal has such a wide range of individual characteristics as a dog. Even within an individual breed of dog there are differences and to the owner, their dog is totally unique. When a prospective owner goes along to choose a puppy or a rescue dog, they usually view several dogs and then make their selection. The dog is then set apart for that owner and prepared.

When Jak was twelve weeks old, we went to a puppy class at the local vets for four consecutive weeks with puppies the same age. Already, most were bigger or fatter or fiercer than Jak. There was another dog named Jak there also, so they were known as 'Big Jak' and 'Little Jak'! The first week, Kevin took him along but after Jak wet on the floor, he refused to go again! Leave it to say, by the fourth and final week, the mop man took to standing beside us, mop and bucket at the ready, ever prepared for the inevitable. Most weeks, little Jak got everything wrong. He trembled under my chair a lot of the time but I didn't care. He was special. He was unique because he was mine.

****

In a similar way, you are a unique child of the Father. If you are a child of God, He set you apart before the foundation of the world to serve Him on this earth and then to rule with Him in the world to come. There is no one quite like you. You have unique fingerprints and a unique DNA. There is no one who looks exactly like you and no one who can live the life He has called you to live. He has called you to be His child. He has set you apart.

Question:

Do you feel you are fulfilling God's calling on your life however grand or humble that may be? How?

Prayer:

Ask God to give you the courage, motivation and anointing to be all He has created you to be.

Meditation:

Psalm 4:3a *But know that the Lord has set apart for Himself him who is godly; the Lord will hear when I call to him.*

Other:

None

Further study:

You are *Honoured:* Psalm 91:15

Notes:

26

You are *Heard*

*(Heard = take in sounds through
the ears; receive news or information etc...)*

Can dogs communicate? If you live with a dog you will tell me that if a dog could talk then it wouldn't need to, because you usually know exactly what it wants. A dog has many ways of letting you know just what he's saying using no words at all.

A dog will use its body and a whole range of sounds to send a signal about its emotions, intentions, needs and desires. Tail, mouth, ears, eyes, nose, head, body and even eyebrow ridges are used to very good effect, as too are barks, howls, growls, whimpers and whines!

We see erect, attentive or laid back submissive ears, sleepy or stressful yawns or a smiling, happy-to-play panting mouth. We see aggressive lips pulled back or feel a friendly lick of greeting. We see raised eyebrow ridges suggesting interest, uncertain lowered brows or affectionate narrowed eyes.

We see a need for attention with stamping front feet, or a desire for an object with pawing and scratching and we witness a head on one side that denotes curiosity or a strange sound in earshot or a recognizable word.

Barks come in a whole variety of types... excited, playful, lonely, fearful, aggressive or distressed. Whether warning growls, miserable howls, whines of request or whimpers of pain, all are used in their desire to communicate with man.

When Kevin is away, if I awaken at 3am to the dog listening intently and growling, then I take notice. I give that attention even if it's only to look out of the window and go back to sleep.

Sitting at his food bowl, standing at the door, a yelp, tail between his legs looking ashamed, a growl, wagging his tail, rolling on his back, I know what he wants. Sitting at the fridge, listening, head on one side, whining from his dog cage, dropping his ball at my feet, staring intently into the dark, I hear him.

If you own a dog, you can fill in the words yourself...He calls and we hear. That's what owners do.

****

God hears what you say. But He also hears what you don't say just as clearly. The Bible says He hears the cry of your heart, He hears the faintest whisper and He hears your silent prayer. He hears your heart beat from excitement and He hears your weary sigh. He is a Father who knows what you need before you speak it. How great is our God?

Question:

Has a desire of your heart ever come to pass before you've prayed?

Prayer:

Thank Him for those times.

Meditation:

Psalm 10:17 *Lord, you have heard the desire of the humble; you will prepare their heart; you will cause your ear to hear.*

Other:

Psalm 4:3b, 5:3, 6:8, 18:6, 34:4, 34:15, 34:17, 38:15, 40:1, 55:17, 102:19-20, 145:19

Further study:

You are *Understood:* Psalm 139:2

Notes:

27

You are Blessed

*(Blessed = make sacred or holy;
bring God's favour on a person or thing)*

There's nothing in the world like a visit to grandma's house, and for a dog it's just the same!

From time to time, we were unable to take Jak along with us on our trips and on one occasion he went to stay with his grandma in Derby. Kevin's mum is a wonderful mother-in-law and an even better grandma. I should have realised he was in for a good time by the inquisition I received on arrival.

What time does he like his breakfast, elevenses, lunch, afternoon snack, evening meal and supper? Does he like to sleep with a hot water bottle or without? Is he covered up to sleep? Should his blanket be checked halfway through the night? And was I sure two packets of treats would be enough for the week? I'm sure I visibly saw Jak's eyes light up while we were talking.

I rang the first time the next morning to give her some information for Kevin. "Jak's still asleep," said Kevin's mum. I eyed the clock. It was 9.30am. "I have buttered toast squares cut up ready for when he gets up," she continued. "Should I wake him or let him lie?" Knowing my dog would still be there at midday, if she let him, I suggested she maybe begin to rouse him fairly soon.

Two days later I rang her again for another reason. "We're having a great time," Kevin's mum recounted. "I've been exceptionally busy since you left." I couldn't think what she could have been doing, so I asked. "Well, I've been stuffing pasta." "Stuffing what?" I repeated. "You left me pasta and chicken for Jak's meals but I thought he would enjoy it much more, and eat more pasta if I stuffed it with the chicken. The only problem is that it takes me an hour to stuff it and it takes him a minute to eat it. It's all I've been doing all day!" she continued. I suddenly had a mental image of my dog, sitting back on a dog-sized deckchair, legs crossed, newspaper in paws, liver flavoured Pina Colada by his side and a cigar chew stick protruding from his mouth! "Would he ever come home again?" I thought.

"I've solved the problem in the bedroom," she concluded before I rang off. "It was too squashed with two of us in a single bed last night so no problem," she finished. "Tonight, I'll sleep in the chair."

I wish I was that dog!

****

God loves to bless His children. Not for what they do or don't do, but because they're His kids. Many times we read that His blessing is on His children so it's important that we begin to thank Him for that and begin to expect those blessings to come. It's good also to take time to thank Him for the things that we might miss too, such as the sunrise, a friendship or a good night's sleep. He delights to bless His children so start to look out for them and then become the blessing in someone else's life.

Question:

Who are you going to come into contact with today (or tomorrow)? How can you become the blessing in their lives?

Prayer:

Pray for the people you will meet and pray God will show you how to be a blessing in their lives.

Meditation:

Psalm 3:8 *Salvation belongs to the Lord. Your blessing is upon Your people.*

Other:

Psalm 2:12b, 21:3, 21:6, 24:5, 29:11, 34:8, 40:4, 84:4, 84:12, 107:38, 85:12, 89:15, 106:3, 112:2, 115:12, 126:3, 128:4, 145:16

Further study:

You are **Prospered:** Psalm 25:13, 35:27

You are **Favoured:** Psalm 5:12, 30:5, 30:7, 36:8, 85:12, 89:17

You are **Shown Kindness:** Psalm 36:10, 40:11, 42:8, 86:15, 92:2, 103:4, 117:2,

Notes:

28

You are *Answered*

(Answer = give or find an
answer to; reply; respond to a signal)

It is said that terriers have a strong propensity to bark. That tended to be the case with Jak and what I discovered was that there was no volume control for these enthusiastic barking sessions. What he discovered was that a little bark can have a big effect. For example, to his delight when the Doberman opposite walked past the house on his daily walk, wee Jak only had to do his biggest squeaky bark and the Doberman left...easy really!!

The 'bark' facility also seemed to have its own timing device. 'Owner being in the bath' seemed to activate it well, as did 'speaking to someone on the telephone' and in fact anything which deprived puppy of attention!

Dogs bark. It helps them to get what they want. Among other things, they are telling you something, communicating with other dogs or expressing an emotion. Dogs bark when they are hungry, sad, bored, lonely or sick. When Kevin goes away, as soon as he leaves, Jak attempts to become the pack leader and for a while he barks at doors, curtains, noises, no noises, the TV, stuffed toys, the fridge and anything else that catches his attention. Luckily, within a few minutes he obviously feels he has asserted his authority in the house and calms down.

Persistence is a great gift which dogs possess in abundance and my dog is no different. He calls and in one way or another, I answer and if I don't, he calls again. I generally always answer. The answer is not always what he wants to hear. It's 'yes', with real enthusiasm, to a wee outside, 'yes' to doggie tricks and walks, and barking at intruders. But it's 'no' to bones in bed, burying next door's cat, and picking fights with other dogs. 'No' to chocolate, coffee, eating poo, rolling in fox droppings, trying to push me out of bed and opening our presents on Christmas Eve after everyone has gone to bed. But there's also a third reply I give, and that's 'wait'. It's 'wait' for your dinner, at busy roads, at the open door, and when approaching big dogs.

I say 'yes', 'no' and 'wait' but it's all for his good. He doesn't always understand but then of course, I know best!

****

That's exactly what God says. To some of our cries, He replies 'yes', to some, He says 'no' and to some, the answer is 'not yet' but it will come. God is not a push button machine where we insert the request and out comes the requirement. He is not a servant who caters for our every whim and He is not an over indulgent parent who spoils His kid without thought. He answers 'yes,' 'no' and 'wait' but it's all for our good. We don't always understand but then of course, He knows best.

Question:

When has God said 'yes,' 'no' and 'wait' in your life?

Prayer:

Thank God that He always answers, even when we don't get our own way all the time. Thank Him that all things work together for good to those that love Him and are called according to His purpose.

Meditation:

Psalm 138:3 *In the day when I cried out, You answered me, and made me bold with strength in my soul.*

Other:

Psalm 20:1, 86:7, 118:5, 118:21

Further study:

Now choose more Bible verses which share how God answers His children.

Notes:

29

You are Shown *Faithfulness*

(Faithful = loyal and trustworthy)

Jak's greatest (and some would say his only) achievement was his graduation from puppy class. Puppy class had been an adventure for us all.

The four weeks progressed nicely and the very last week of the course included the 'agility' test. Being part Yorkie, this was a strong point and I was quietly confident. As expected, Jak sailed through the first three activities of walking up a bench, jumping over a stick and stepping through a hoop. There was only the tunnel left and he would be champion of the week. Stopwatch at the ready, Little Jak poised to start while Big Jak, and the rest of the dogs looked on. The room was quiet with anticipation. Everyone knew that he was ahead on points. At the starting whistle, Little Jak approached the first chair, went through it no problem and did the same with the second and third. Now, only the tunnel left. In an instant, he disappeared into the plastic tunnel as though he had done it a thousand times. My pride grew by the second! The room held its breath, knowing that the finishing line was one metre from where he was to emerge. Five seconds, ten seconds…twenty seconds…no Jak. Fifty seconds…one minute. Eventually, I tentatively approached the exit of the tunnel, to see Jak fulfilling his terrier hunting and tunnelling instincts, quite happy to stay there for the rest of the evening.

Eventually, we had to pick up the end of the tunnel with Jak, four legs asplayed and eyes determined, firmly hanging on to the tunnel sides, and shake him out! By this time Jak was definitely ranking last but he gave the doggy training class a very comical week to end with!

Actually, I often wondered…was it us training him or the other way round? I was never quite sure and it certainly tests the patience when he cries to go out in the middle of the night in the depths of winter. But it's very hard to be angry as he licks my cheek and curls up and goes to sleep on my lap. He may be a pain at times but we love him, he is our dog and we are so pleased he is part of our lives.

****

God is so faithful. He is the one person who will always be the same, will never leave your side and who in the midst of a continually changing world is someone you can rely upon. In this world of constant change, moral decline and increasing natural disasters He will be faithful to you. While visiting the earthquake hit region of Christchurch, New Zealand, we witnessed Him right there with His people. Staying in the gang ridden land of Mexico, He is there with His people. Walking through the sin filled streets of Bankok, He is there with His people. And wherever you may be, He will be faithful to you, both today and every day of your life.

Question:

How has God been faithful to you?

Prayer:

Begin to thank Him for those things then pray for those who need to know His faithfulness today

Meditation:

Psalm 37:3 *Trust in the Lord, and do good. Dwell in the land and feed on His faithfulness.*

Other:

Psalm 92:2, 119:90

Further study:

Now choose more Bible verses which speak about God's faithfulness to you.

Notes:

30

You are
Strengthened

(Strengthen = make or become stronger)

Jak is a puppy no longer. The days of the bundle of fur on legs have long gone.

It's funny how soon you forget puppyhood...worrying that your dog might piddle on someone else's carpet, pulling stuff out of his back end which you've seen disappear down his throat the day before, sleepless nights while trying to insist he sleeps downstairs, racing round the garden/house/furniture (him not me) then dropping and sleeping for hours on end (well, maybe me too), barking at traffic cones and daddy longlegs and people with uniforms like policemen, running off with unmentionables, being sick in my handbag, chasing the cat down the road, eating live spiders and a ten pound note, running away from the sweeping brush and growling at his reflection in the mirror...

He has given up barking at clouds. He's not sure why they go away but he seems to know it's not because he barks at them! He's

127

become a sophisticated people watcher, understanding your facial expression, tone of voice and body position. He's graduated from his in-car training and he's survived his time at weekly dog camp. He's even trying hard to conquer his 'small dog syndrome' though I have a feeling that 'little dog' attitude may be a long time in leaving!

Jak is growing and changing and being strengthened every day. And I'm glad he is. Can you imagine having an eternal puppy?

****

From the moment we commit our lives to God and desire that He becomes part of our daily experience, He commits Himself to a strengthening of us as people. As a mother does not expect a baby to strengthen itself, but feeds and clothes, nurtures and teaches her child, so too our God commits Himself to our best interests in bringing those things into our lives which will mould us, build us up and strengthen us.

Question:

What things in your own life have you seen strengthened over the last few years? What are you aware of that still needs to become stronger?

Prayer:

Ask God to make you stronger in that area.

Meditation:

Psalm 18:39 *For you have armed me with strength for the battle; You have subdued under me those who rose up against me.*

Other:

Psalm 18:32, 18:39, 20:2, 23:3, 27:1, 27:14, 28:7, 29:11, 31:4, 31:24, 37:39, 41:3, 46:1, 68:28, 71:16, 89:17, 105:4, 118:14

Further study:

You are **Revived:** Psalm 138:7

You are **Restored:** Psalm 23:3

You are **Sustained:** Psalm 55:22

Notes:

31

You are *Redeemed*

(Redeemed = 1. Buy something back;
pay off a debt 2. Save a person from
damnation 3. Make up for faults)

My mind wandered back to the past and for a minute, I was with them again. With Jock, my very first dog, and I was a child again running through the grass, with him by my side.

With Michael, as newly married, we tucked him into my raincoat, along with the little collar and lead we'd bought for the event, warm from the cold wind. We brought him into our home and we watched him grow into a young strong dog and fill our home with smiles and good things.

I closed my eyes and pictured Mary, a podgy bundle of fur when she arrived and then very soon, a growing bundle of mischief, eyes sparkling and mouth open, grinning as dogs do. I opened my eyes and smiled to myself. She was funny. She made us laugh.

I then looked down at wee Jak Mac Peat, yes definitely a 'big personality in a small package' as they say, and I knew that as long as I lived, I would see him there, eyes bright, tail wagging. I bent down and lifted him close, more for my sake than his.

In monetary terms, they were worth nothing – they weren't show dogs or even pedigrees. But in my terms, they were worth thousands. I had bought them all at a very small price but the gift I received each time was a lifetime of something priceless.

Thinking back to the many dogs we have loved and lost, they became amazing creatures who have travelled the journey from their own species into the hearts and lives of man. They brought life and love and laughter into our everyday existence. They taught us about ourselves and about others and about God. They brought out the child in us, the parent and also the responsibility of adulthood. They taught us to rest and to play, to be persistent but patient. They modelled taking each day as it comes, living with no regrets and valuing everyone regardless of status. They lived to enrich our existence, to be totally devoted and to love unconditionally. We know they have enriched our lives beyond measure.

****

And when I thought about it I knew too, that whatever I felt about them, that my Father God felt that about me and much, much more. You too, have been bought with a price but not only that, He actually paid the debt of your sin and saved you too...and not just for a lifetime, but for the whole of eternity. Whoever you are, wherever you are, He truly, truly loves you.

Question:

Do you truly appreciate what God did for you? Wherever you are on that journey, ask Him to make His gift of redemption to you, clearer and clearer as every day goes by.

Prayer:

Thank Him that you, yes you, were bought with a price, that your debts were paid and that you were saved from an eternity of punishment to a future in heaven for ever. Now pray for others in your life wherever they are on that journey.

Meditation:

Psalm 49:15 *But God will redeem my soul from the power of the grave, for He shall receive me.*

Other:

Psalm 31:5, 34:22, 55:18, 103:4, 130:7

Further study:

You are *Saved:* Psalm 34:6, 34:18, 91:16, 109:30-31, 116:6, 118:14, 118:21, 138:7, 149:4

Notes:

Prayer:

If you've never actually begun a relationship with God and after reading this book you are beginning to wonder if there is a Father in Heaven. If you're beginning to wonder if there is a God who you need to get to know, then use the prayer below to start a new chapter in your life.

"Dear God,

You know all about me. You know that I'm not even sure you exist. Yet you love me all the same. Today, I want to join your family and become your child.

I confess my wrong doing and bring it to your cross.

I ask you to forgive those things and I ask you to clean up my life.

I acknowledge that you sent your Son to die on a cross to save me from hell and give me a life in heaven.

I ask today that you become my Lord and I ask you to begin a new chapter in my life.

In Jesus' name

Amen."

But now ask the beasts, and they will teach you;
And the birds of the air, and they will tell you.

Job 12:7

Remembering

Rene Peat

1927-2012

Previous books by Margaret Peat

The White Elephant contains eleven real life stories from daily life in Glasgow, which highlight various issues of the heart. The chapters deal with the subjects of forgiveness, forgiving yourself, repentance, shame, a heart of stone, inferiority, loss, fear, finding perspective in problems, the Father's love and being special to God.

The Seagull contains eleven more true stories which continue to highlight various issues of the heart. The chapters deal with the subjects of attitude, ungodly beliefs, making choices, the power of words, generational influences, putting God in a box, the place of mercy, soaking, sowing and reaping, performance orientation and breaking out of your comfort zone.

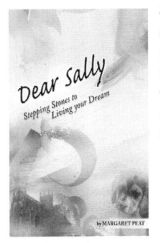

Dear Sally contains 34 letters sent to a special friend. These letters illustrate some very important and challenging life-truths. As we put them into practise, these principles can take us nearer to living that dream.

These books have been highly commended by Christian leaders and those who have read them. If you would like to obtain a copy of either of these books or have more information concerning them, then please contact KMPeat@aol.com or www.elimscotland.org.uk.